IS THE LORD'S DAY
FOR YOU?

✕ CULTIVATING BIBLICAL GODLINESS

Series Editors

Joel R. Beeke and Ryan M. McGraw

Dr. D. Martyn Lloyd-Jones once said that what the church needs to do most of all is "to begin herself to live the Christian life. If she did that, men and women would be crowding into our buildings. They would say, 'What is the secret of this?'" As Christians, one of our greatest needs is for the Spirit of God to cultivate biblical godliness in us in order to put the beauty of Christ on display through us, all to the glory of the triune God. With this goal in mind, this series of booklets treats matters vital to Christian experience at a basic level. Each booklet addresses a specific question in order to inform the mind, warm the affections, and transform the whole person by the Spirit's grace, so that the church may adorn the doctrine of God our Savior in all things.

IS THE LORD'S DAY
FOR YOU?

JOSEPH A. PIPA JR.

REFORMATION HERITAGE BOOKS
GRAND RAPIDS, MICHIGAN

Is the Lord's Day for You?
© 2016 by Joseph A. Pipa Jr.

Reformation Heritage Books
2965 Leonard St. NE
Grand Rapids, MI 49525
616-977-0889 / Fax 616-285-3246
orders@heritagebooks.org
www.heritagebooks.org

Printed in the United States of America
16 17 18 19 20 21/10 9 8 7 6 5 4 3 2 1

ISBN 978-1-60178-485-8

IS THE LORD'S DAY
FOR YOU?

Not merely a system of doctrine, Reformed Christianity has always offered an approach to how believers ought to live. Reformed piety springs directly from Reformed thinking, and this piety includes the centrality of the church, family worship and instruction, strict adherence to God's moral law, and God-centered worship. Foundational to this piety is the concept that the Lord's Day is the Christian Sabbath, which we are to sanctify by acts of public and private worship as well as deeds of Christian service.

Today, however, many believers question whether the Bible actually requires Christians to observe one day in seven. Assuming that all days are equal, they think that designating Sunday for worship is merely a matter of the church's need to have an agreed-on day for worship. Growing numbers of people are repudiating the idea that Sunday is the Christian Sabbath.[1]

Historically, the Reformation standards, such as the Westminster Standards and the Heidelberg Catechism, have described purposes and uses for the Lord's Day, which are different from much of the contemporary practice of the church. So how should we view the Lord's Day today? Does God expect us to view it differently from the other days of the week? Once a person has worshiped, is he free to spend the day as he pleases? Is it really sin for us to work at our jobs, go shopping, and eat at restaurants on the Lord's Day? In the past, Christians stopped normal working and recreational activities to devote themselves to spiritual pursuits on the Lord's Day, viewing the day as a means of grace. Do we see it that way now? Does the Bible give a clear answer on how we are to observe the Lord's Day? Is the Lord's Day for you?

TEMPORARY OR PERMANENT?

In Deuteronomy 5, Moses reminds the Israelites of the Ten Commandments God had given His people

---

1. For different views, see Christopher Donato, ed., *Perspectives on the Sabbath* (Nashville: B&H Publishing Group, 2011). For the view expressed in this booklet, see Ryan M. McGraw, *The Day of Worship: Reassessing the Christian Life in Light of the Sabbath* (Grand Rapids: Reformation Heritage Books, 2011); and Joseph Pipa, *The Lord's Day* (Fern, Ross-shire, Scotland: Christian Focus Publication, 1997).

at Mount Sinai. The fourth commandment requires that God's people

> keep the sabbath day to sanctify it, as the LORD thy God hath commanded thee. Six days thou shalt labour, and do all thy work: but the seventh day is the sabbath of the LORD thy God: in it thou shalt not do any work, thou, nor thy son, nor thy daughter, nor thy manservant, nor thy maidservant, nor thine ox, nor thine ass, nor any of thy cattle, nor thy stranger that is within thy gates; that thy manservant and thy maidservant may rest as well as thou. (vv. 12–14)

It is clear that the fourth commandment requires a careful observance of the Sabbath. The question is whether this commandment was a temporary, ceremonial law given only for Israel or a permanent, moral law given for all people. In the Bible there are temporary laws called positive laws and permanent laws called moral laws.

A positive law is a commandment of God that is not morally necessary, meaning that the thing commanded in and of itself is not inherently right or wrong. God requires or forbids certain things for the immediate and temporary needs of His people and their relationship to Him in the same way that parents adapt and even change rules for their children as the children grow older. Positive laws are binding only on the people or, as in the case of Israel, the nation to whom they were given. For example, the prohibition to Adam and Eve not to eat of the fruit of the Tree of the Knowledge of Good and Evil was a positive law. There was nothing inherently holy about eating or not eating; rather, the prohibition was the means God chose to test their willingness to obey Him (Gen. 2:16–17). The ceremonial laws of the Mosaic covenant are also examples of positive law.

A moral law, on the other hand, is a commandment that reflects the moral nature of God and our relation to Him and one another. Moral laws are absolutely required of and are permanently binding on all people. "Thou shalt not kill" is an example of a moral law (Deut. 5:17). Murder is wrong not only because God's Word prohibits it, but also because it is inherently evil. "Thou shalt not kill" is a permanently binding obligation on all people in all ages (Deut. 5:17). Although there are temporary aspects involved in Old Testament Sabbath observance (more about this below), the principle of a special day devoted to the worship and service of God is a perpetually binding moral obligation (Westminster Confession of Faith 21.7).

INSTITUTING THE LORD'S DAY

To understand the perpetual nature of Lord's Day observance we begin with God's institution of the Sabbath in Genesis 2:1–3. Along with the mandate to work (Gen. 1:28; 2:15) and the institution of marriage (Gen. 2:18–25), God instituted the Sabbath to govern the lives of all mankind. Like the ordinances of work and marriage, the Sabbath ordinance is permanent.[2]

God instituted the Sabbath both by His example and by the words of institution. First, He established the principle of Sabbath-keeping by resting on the seventh day: "And on the seventh day God ended his work which he had made; and he rested on the seventh day from all his work which he had made" (Gen. 2:2). The term "Sabbath" is derived from the word "rested" in verse 2. By resting on the seventh day of creation, God Himself established the principle and practice of Sabbath observance. In order to understand the Sabbath ordinance, first we need to understand why God rested.

God rested on the seventh day of creation for three reasons. First, by resting God declared that His work as Creator was completed. In Genesis 2:1, God pronounces the completion of His work as Creator: "Thus the heavens and the earth were finished, and all the host of them." The words "heavens," "earth," and "host" encompass all the products of God's creative work on days 1 through 6.

God's rest, however, was not a cessation from all work. Jesus confirms this when He says in John 5:17, "My Father worketh hitherto, and I work." God continues to work in providence and especially in

---

2. For a discussion of these creation ordinances, see John Murray, *Principles of Conduct: Aspects of Biblical Ethics* (Grand Rapids: Eerdmans, 1964), 27–106.

redemption. From eternity, He decreed the salvation of His elect. Since the fall, He has been working to accomplish that salvation. He redeemed Israel, delivering them from the bondage of Egypt; He has established His church; and in the greatest deed of all He became a man and lived on the earth in order to accomplish redemption. To this day He continues to work by calling His people unto Himself and justifying, adopting, sanctifying, and keeping them. Hence, God did not rest from all His work, but only the work of creation.

Since He continues to work, why does He place this emphasis on rest? When God rested from the work of creation, He declared that He had completed the work of creation exactly as He intended. This truth is demonstrated in the constant refrain in Genesis 1 of "it was so." Never again would there be a need for His work of fiat, instantaneous creation. It is finished! He bids us to worship Him as Creator of heaven and earth (Rev. 4:11).

Second, God rested to express the delight He took in His creation. Moses amplifies this concept in Exodus 31:17: "[The Sabbath] is a sign between me and the children of Israel forever: for in six days the LORD made heaven and earth, and on the seventh day he rested, and was refreshed." What a delightful phrase—"he rested, and was refreshed." What does it mean? Did God need to rest because He was weary or tired? No, we know that He had not grown weary with His work of creation for He is omnipotent and unchangeable. He is the same yesterday, today, and forever. As Isaiah says, He "fainteth not, neither is weary" (40:28). Certainly God did not need to rest because His creative work wearied Him.

On the seventh day, God experienced a refreshment of joy as He contemplated the beauty and the perfection of all He had done. At the conclusion of the sixth day, "God saw every thing that he had made, and, behold, it was very good" (Gen. 1:31). On the seventh day God surveyed His work and took great pleasure in what He had made. Just as you step back to contemplate with joy something you have built or accomplished, God stepped back (so to speak) to contemplate His work with pleasure.

Third, by resting on the seventh day, God pictured the rest He would provide for man. He offered Adam and his descendants life (eternal rest). If Adam had not fallen into sin, he would have entered into that rest without passing through death. By resting on the seventh day, God pictured the promised rest.

By God's grace, He did not cancel the offer of rest after the fall. Rather, God renewed the promise of life, not through Adam's obedience but through a redeemer. According to His eternal purpose, the day of rest became a weekly promise and reminder to sinners that God would provide redemption and rest.

By resting, God gave us an example, reminding us that He is the all-powerful Creator who completed His work and thus has authority and power to govern it. He calls us to seek our rest in Him as we contemplate His goodness and grace in the beauty of creation and the wonderful offer of redemption. In our Sabbath resting, we are reminded that God's works of creation and redemption are finished, and thus we praise Him; we contemplate the complex beauty of His works and are refreshed in communion with Him; and we anticipate our eternal life with Him.

CONSECRATING THE LORD'S DAY

Having taught these things by His rest, God formally consecrated the seventh day for man to follow Him in keeping the Lord's Day. In addition to giving us the example of His rest, He *blessed* the day and *sanctified* it: "God blessed the seventh day, and sanctified it: because that in it he had rested from all his work which God created and made" (Gen. 2:3). In this dual action of blessing and sanctifying the day, God instituted the pattern of six days of work and a seventh day of sacred rest.

Blessing the Day

By blessing the day, God assigned it special purpose. In the creation account, when God blessed something He established purpose and endowed the thing created with the ability to fulfill that purpose. For example, when God blessed the animals in Genesis 1:22, He established their purpose of multiplying and filling the earth and endowed them with the desire and ability to procreate so that they might accomplish this purpose. Similarly, in Genesis 1:28, He blessed man, giving him the purpose of multiplying, filling the earth, and ruling over it. By means of this blessing, God endowed man with the desire and ability to fulfill this task.

In like manner, when God blessed the seventh day, He gave it purpose and the ability to fulfill that purpose. He appointed the seventh day, the day He entered into His rest, to be a weekly pattern for the observance of His rest. Furthermore, He promised He would bless those who would follow His example of rest every seventh day. So by blessing the day, He made the day a blessing for man. Surely Christ had this in mind when He said, "The sabbath was made for man, and not man for the sabbath" (Mark 2:27).

Sanctifying the Day
God's purpose in blessing the day stands out more clearly when we understand what it means that He "sanctified" the day. By this act, He declared the day to be holy. When God sanctified something, He separated it from its common use for special use connected with His worship and service. For example, He declared to be holy or sanctified the garments of the priest, the altar, the sanctuary, and all the furnishings and utensils used in the tabernacle, and, later the temple. On account of this sanctification these things could be used only for the holy purposes of worship (for a particular example, look at Exodus 30:37–38).

How then do we apply this sanctification to the seventh day? We conclude that in the same way God set aside certain things for His special use and service, He also set aside the seventh day for the special purpose of worship and service. This does not deny that the other six days are holy and are to be used for God's glory; Christians are to glorify God in all of life (Rom. 12:1–2; cf. Westminster Shorter Catechism 1). God, though, establishes the seventh day as a holy day for special purposes.

A Perpetually Binding Moral Obligation

By blessing and sanctifying the day, God communicated to Adam and Eve, and through the Scripture to us, the principle of keeping the Lord's Day holy. We are to treat as holy what God declares to be holy. We may conclude that the observation of one day out of seven is a perpetually binding moral obligation based on this creation ordinance (Westminster Confession of Faith 21.7).

Turning to the fourth commandment (Ex. 20:8–11), we note that God gives Genesis 2:2–3 as the ground for the moral obligation to keep the Sabbath day holy. In verse 11 He states, "For in six days the LORD made heaven and earth, the sea, and all that in them is, and rested the seventh day: wherefore the LORD blessed the sabbath day, and hallowed it." The fourth commandment is the precise formulation and practical amplification of the creation ordinance of Genesis 2:1–3.

Some, however, suggest that the fourth commandment is ceremonial because God declared it to be a sign of the Mosaic covenant (Ex. 31:16–17). For a number of reasons, though, the fourth commandment is a moral and not a ceremonial law. The first reason is the unity of the Ten Commandments. These commandments, which were given in such an awesome manner at Mount Sinai and were engraved by God's finger in stone, stand together as a unit. It is against all sound reason to isolate one by saying that it is ceremonial and no longer binding.

This unity is all the more evident when we consider the relationship of the first four laws. The first four function together as a whole, summarized in Deuteronomy and by our Savior (Deut. 6:5; Matt. 22:37) as the great commandment. The first commandment tells us that God alone is to be worshiped; the second instructs us how He is to be worshiped; the third sets forth the attitude of the worshiper; while the fourth dictates that there is to be a day devoted to that worship.

The second reason, as already noted, is that God bases the fourth commandment on the creation ordinance. Like marriage and work, this is a perpetually binding moral obligation.

Third, note that God not only refers to the obligation of the covenant people to keep the Sabbath but also to the responsibility of the stranger not to work (Ex. 20:10). The stranger was the person outside the covenant who chose to live in the midst of God's people. Even though he was not in the covenant and could not take part in the feasts or in the sacrifices, God obligated him to keep the Sabbath. As he was obligated to keep other commandments, he was obligated not to work on the Sabbath (Neh. 13:15–21).

Therefore, there are many sound reasons for maintaining that the fourth commandment is a moral and not a ceremonial law. This is not a denial that there are ceremonial aspects involved in the fourth commandment. Each of the Ten Commandments has ceremonial and judicial applications. The Ten Words summarize man's moral responsibility to God. The judicial laws applied the moral laws to the civic life of Israel, while the ceremonial laws applied the moral law to Israel's worship.

For example, the second commandment, which forbids making graven images and bowing down to them, applies to the entire system of tabernacle/ temple worship, sacrifices, and religious festivals. As types of Christ, all these elements of worship would pass away. But the moral principles of the second commandment remain.

The fourth commandment, therefore, contains ceremonial aspects—festivals, new moons, and Sabbaths. These aspects applied exclusively to Israel, and, because Christ fulfilled them, He abrogated them (Col. 2:16–17). The principle, however, that God would have man devote a whole day to worship and religious service is woven into the moral fabric of the universe.

Certainly there is no tension between the permanent, moral obligation of the fourth commandment and the fact that it was appointed as a sign of the covenant between God and the children of Israel (Ex. 31:16–17). The moral obligation in its seventh-day cycle would distinguish the old covenant people from all the other nations of the earth. For this reason, redemption from Egypt is given as the ground for the Sabbath in Deuteronomy 5:15. God is not replacing the creation ordinance as the basis for the commandment when He first gave it at Mount Sinai. Rather, God adds a second reason for Sabbath-keeping for Israel as His covenant people. They were to keep the Sabbath because they had been redeemed. As such, Sabbath-keeping had a distinct covenantal role. But this role never exhausted the initial purpose of the Sabbath.

Indeed, God gave the Jews the seventh-day Sabbath as a memorial of redemption. Since the redemption from Egypt, however, pictured the greater redemption accomplished by Christ, the memorial day of the former promised the latter. As Paul says in Colossians 2:17, the seventh-day Sabbath pointed to the Savior to come. Taking all these things into consideration, then, the evidence is clear that the fourth commandment, though containing a ceremonial element, is a perpetually binding moral obligation for all people.

CHANGE OF DAY

But since the fourth commandment specifies the seventh day, are we not compelled either to keep the seventh day holy or to admit that the fourth commandment is dated and no longer binding? No, because, as we have seen, the fourth commandment had ceremonial aspects. The Westminster Confession (21.7) refers to the Sabbath law as positive and moral. This means that the moral law of Sabbath-keeping had positive elements—namely, how often and which day. Because the particular day is a positive law, the day can be changed without affecting the moral nature of the law. As the Westminster Confession says about the day: "From the beginning of the world to the resurrection of Christ, [it] was the last day of the week; and, from the resurrection of Christ, was changed into the first day of the week, which in Scripture is called the Lord's Day, and is to be continued to the end of the world, as the Christian Sabbath" (21.7).

Some suggest that although the principle of the Christian Sabbath remains, the church may choose whatever day it prefers to observe it. They refer to Paul's prohibitions concerning days in Romans 14:5–6; Galatians 4:9–10; and Colossians 2:16–17. We learn from the context of these passages that Paul is dealing with Jewish practices, not with the moral obligation to keep holy one day in seven, but rather with the religious observance of various Jewish holy days. He makes this clear by the terms he uses in

Colossians 2:16, "an holyday, or of the new moon, or of the sabbath days." These three terms are often used together to describe the special holy days of Jewish worship (see 2 Chron. 8:13; 31:3; Lev. 23:1–25). Some Jewish Christians sought to maintain these days in addition to the New Testament Sabbath. Paul countered that they were free to do so for a brief period until the destruction of the temple in AD 70, but they could not obligate others. Therefore, Paul abrogates the seventh-day Sabbath and forbids the church to require a day by its own authority.

That we may not apply Paul's prohibition about days to the New Testament Sabbath is clear because the New Testament church worshiped on the first day of the week (Acts 20:7; 1 Cor. 16:1–2). The apostle John highlighted the special character of the day by the title the "Lord's day" (Rev. 1:10). The term "Lord's" is the same used to distinguish the sacramental meal, Communion, from all other meals. Paul calls it the "Lord's supper" (1 Cor. 11:20).

By divine warrant, the church began to worship on the first day of the week as a memorial to Christ's resurrection and His declaration that by His death and resurrection He purchased eternal rest for His people. We have begun to partake of God's rest and will fully enter into it when our Savior returns. The writer of Hebrews develops this theme in Hebrews 4:9–10: "There remaineth therefore a rest to the people of God. For he that is entered into his rest, he also hath ceased from his own works, as God did from his." The term "rest" in this passage literally means a "Sabbath-keeping." In other words, the New Testament church is to keep a Sabbath day.[3] The word translated "Sabbath rest" (*sabbatismos*) is uniquely used only this time in the Bible.

Although the noun form of the word used in Hebrews 4:9 is found nowhere else in the Bible, the verb form of the word (*sabbatizo*) is used a number of times in the Septuagint (the Greek translation of the Old Testament). The first use of the verb form is in Exodus 16:30: "So the people rested [*sabbatized*] on the seventh day"; that is, they observed a Sabbath rest. This verse concludes the section in which God tells them not to collect manna on the seventh day because it is the Sabbath (16:29). When the people obeyed God and kept the Sabbath, they *sabbatized*.

This idea of Sabbath-keeping is involved every time the verb is used. For example, after a description of some feasts that were part of the worship of God's people, Leviticus 23:32 says, "It shall be unto you a sabbath of rest, and ye shall afflict your souls; in the ninth day of the month at even, from even unto even, shall ye celebrate your sabbath." The phrase "celebrate your Sabbath" is *sabbatizo*.

So we see from the passage in Hebrews that the theology of redemption accomplished does not annul a continued Sabbath-keeping, but requires it. And although we do not need a reinforcement or

---

3. For a defense of this position see Pipa, *Lord's Day*, 113–16.

repetition of an Old Testament moral command, God gives clear new covenant instruction since the Sabbath did have ceremonial and typical significance. What better book to reiterate Sabbath observance than Hebrews, which teaches most clearly how all Old Testament ceremonial worship practices were fulfilled in Christ and therefore repealed.[4]

In addition to establishing the principle that there remains a present Sabbath-keeping, Hebrews 4:9–10 also establishes the day of that Sabbath observance. Verse 10 gives the grounds and explanation for verse 9. Notice that the writer connects verse 9 to verse 10 with "for," which means "because." There remains a Sabbath-keeping "for he that is entered into his rest, he also hath ceased from his own works, as God did from his."

In verse 10, the writer compares Christ's rest from His work of redemption with God's rest from the work of creation. Many commentators interpret verse 10 to refer to the believer's turning from sin to rest in Christ.[5] The New International Version translates verse 10, "For anyone who enters God's rest also rests from his own work, just as God did from

---

4. A. W. Pink, *An Exposition of Hebrews* (Grand Rapids: Baker, 1967), 1: 210.

5. For example, John Calvin favors this interpretation in his commentary on this verse. Also see A. T. Lincoln, "The Lord's Day: Sabbath and Sunday in the Post-Apostolic Church," in *From Sabbath to Lord's Day: A Biblical, Historical, and Theological Investigation*, ed. D. A. Carson (Grand Rapids: Zondervan, 1982), 213–14.

his." The English Standard Version says, "For whoever has entered God's rest has also rested from his works as God did from his." The King James (and New King James) are closest to the Greek: "For he that is entered into his rest, he also hath ceased from his own works, as God did from his."

John Owen offers three reasons for applying verse 10 to Christ's rest and not the believer's.[6] First, it is improper to compare the believer's rest from sinful works to God's rest from His great work of creation. Moreover, God's rest was one of joy and contemplation while the sinner's rest is one of grief and hatred. Owen's second argument involves the change of pronoun. Throughout Hebrews 3:7–4:11, the writer refers to the rest of the believer in the plural: "Let *us* therefore fear" (4:1); "For *we* which have believed do enter into rest" (4:3); "Let *us* labour therefore" (4:11). But in verse 10, he refers to an individual: "For *he* that is entered" (all emphases added). The use of the singular pronoun suggests someone other than the people of God—that is, an individual who has entered his rest as God has entered His. Third, in verse 10, the writer describes a rest that is already completed, while in verse 11 he makes it quite clear that the responsibility to enter into the rest remains for the believer.

---

6. John Owen, *An Exposition of the Epistle to the Hebrews*, ed. W. H. Goold (Grand Rapids: Baker, 1980), 2:331–36.

Some object, "Why use an indefinite reference to Christ? Is it not awkward to introduce Christ in this fashion?" Actually, Christ and His rest are before readers throughout this section. Remember the exhortation begins in 3:6, "But Christ as a son over his own house; whose house are we, if we hold fast…." Hebrews 4:11 refers to "that rest"—namely, the rest provided by Christ. Furthermore, Hebrews 4:14 reminds us that Christ has entered into His rest. That the entering has occurred in the past along with the impropriety of comparing the believer's rest from dead works with God's rest from creation leave me with no other alternative than to interpret verse 10 in terms of Christ.

This interpretation provides a parallel between the work of creation and the work of redemption. At the conclusion of creation, God rested on the seventh day to declare His work completed, to delight in that work, and to renew the promise of eternal rest.

God the Son rested on the first day of the week as a sign that His work of redemption had objectively been accomplished, and nothing remained to be done. In the resurrection, He entered into the joy of His work and confirmed that eternal life had been purchased. (Isa. 53:10–11; Heb. 12:2) By His example, the day was changed.[7]

---

7. See Geerhardus Vos, *Biblical Theology: Old and New Testaments* (Grand Rapids: Eerdmans, 1968), 158.

KEEPING THE LORD'S DAY

With these things in mind, we need to investigate the role of the fourth commandment in regulating the observance of the Lord's Day. How then should the day be kept? God's purpose in the fourth commandment is to free us from our daily business so that we may do business with Him.

The fourth commandment states the purpose of the Sabbath: "Remember the sabbath day, to keep it holy" (Ex. 20:8). The word "remember" has a two-fold significance. In the first place God is saying, "Do not forget or neglect it." The call to remember the Sabbath teaches that the Sabbath as an institution had already been established; God had already established the Sabbath by a creation ordinance. At creation, He made the day holy, and He exhorts us not to forget that.

In the Bible, however, the term "remember" means more than not forgetting. It also means to observe and celebrate. If you are asked if you remembered your anniversary, the question is not simply whether you remembered the actual date, but what you did to observe the occasion. We "remember" special occasions by giving gifts, going out to dinner, or gathering friends together. When God calls us to remember the Sabbath day, He is commanding us to observe it in a special way—to commemorate it. We "remember" the Sabbath by observing it according to God's regulation. For this reason, when God repeated the Ten Commandments forty years later,

He used the word "observe" instead of "remember." "Keep [or observe] the sabbath day to sanctify it…. Therefore the LORD thy God commanded thee to keep the sabbath day" (Deut. 5:12–15).

When we understand the significance of "remember," we realize that God never intended the day merely for idleness. Some suggest that the sole purpose of the fourth commandment was to provide physical rest for Israel and for us. As God's rest, however, was not a rest of inactivity, the rest commanded by the fourth commandment is not a rest of inactivity, but of holy commemoration. According to Leviticus 23:2–3, Sabbath rest entailed corporate worship:

> Speak unto the children of Israel, and say unto them: Concerning the feasts of the LORD, which ye shall proclaim to be holy convocations, these are my feasts. Six days shall work be done: but the seventh day is the sabbath of rest, an holy convocation; ye shall do no work therein: it is the sabbath of the LORD in all your dwellings.

Properly used, the day enables us to remember God and His saving work. We are to treat the day as holy, sanctifying it as the Westminster Shorter Catechism question 60 teaches:

> The Sabbath is to be sanctified by holy resting all that day, even from such worldly employment and recreation as are lawful on other days, and spending the whole time in the public and private exercises of God's worship, except so

much is to taken up in the works of necessity and mercy.

Some wrongly interpret the Heidelberg Catechism question 103:

What doth God require in the fourth commandment?

First, that the ministry of the gospel and the schools be maintained; and that I, especially on the sabbath, that is, on the day of rest, diligently frequent the church of God, to hear his word, to use the sacraments, publicly to call upon the Lord, and contribute to the relief of the poor. Secondly, that all the days of my life I cease from my evil works, and yield myself to the Lord, to work by his Holy Spirit in me: and thus begin in this life the eternal sabbath.

They claim that the Heidelberg Catechism requires only physical rest and participating in public worship.

The fourth commandment, however, teaches that we rest in order to worship. The cessation from work and recreation prescribed by the fourth commandment frees us to worship. This position is precisely that of Ursinus, one of the framers of the Heidelberg Catechism. He wrote, "All those other works which men ordinarily perform on the other days of the week might on the Sabbath give place to the private and public worship of God."[8]

8. *The Commentary of Dr. Zacharias Ursinus on the Heidelberg Catechism* (Phillipsburg, N.J.: Presbyterian and Reformed, 1985), 558.

Others argue that cessation from regular work is not part of the continuing moral requirement of the fourth commandment because Christ broke the Jewish Sabbath. We know, however, that Christ could not have broken the fourth commandment and fulfilled His role as the Messiah who came to do the will of God (Ps. 40:6–8; Matt. 5:1–20). He violated only the Jewish traditions.[9]

The prohibitions of the fourth commandment teach us how to structure the day in order to derive the most benefit from it (Ex. 20:9–10), showing us how to structure our lives personally, domestically, and socially. Personally, the Lord frees us from our ordinary work: "The seventh day is the sabbath of the LORD thy God: in it thou shalt not do any work" (Ex. 20:10). The term "work" includes all types of work. Verse 9 uses the word "labor," which refers to manual labor—agricultural and other forms of labor performed by the hands. The term "work" is a more comprehensive word that encompasses the work described by "labor" but also includes all business, trading and commerce, and domestic chores. By using both terms, God makes clear that He prohibits all our regular work and activity.

God not only structures our occupational life but also commands us to structure our domestic lives. Addressing us in our roles as parents and guardians,

---

9. For a detailed discussion of Christ and the Sabbath, see Pipa, *Lord's Day*, 68–94.

He includes among those who should not be working "thou, nor thy son, nor thy daughter." As parents we are to structure the lives of our covenant children so that they also may be freed from work in order to devote themselves to the special transactions of the day. We are responsible for providing a positive and proper Sabbath-keeping structure for our children.

This requirement means that we set an example of Sabbath-keeping for our children. Moreover, we are to teach them what they should be doing, helping them to order their lives and schoolwork, and giving them only truly essential chores around the house on the Lord's Day. We use the day as well to teach them that there is greater enjoyment in life than playing. Furthermore, we are to create for them a day they will enjoy and anticipate, not a day that hangs over the week like an ominous, dark cloud.

In addition to being a family responsibility, structuring of the Lord's Day requires a social responsibility. We are to structure the day for others in society for whom we are responsible; namely, those employees who work directly for us as well as those who serve in the public sector. Hence, we need to avoid shopping, unnecessary dining out, and recreational activities that cause others to work on the Lord's Day.[10] It is a weak excuse to argue that res-

---

10. See Pipa, *The Lord's Day*, chapters 10–13 for more detailed suggestions on preparing for and observing the Lord's Day. In this section I am also indebted to remarks by Dr. Ryan McGraw.

taurant and retail workers are going to be working anyway, so it really doesn't matter what we do. You are commanded not to cause others to do unnecessary work. If you use a person's services, you are partly responsible for that person's working on the Lord's Day.

Furthermore, as part of our social responsibility, God commands us to allow our animals to rest; they need rest just as people do. Israel was an agrarian society, and a portion of the necessary work was done by animals. God reminds us that He built into the fabric of creation the need for all living things to rest. Even the land was to rest (see Leviticus 25). Surely it is a fair inference to apply this principle to anything that can wear out. Just as employees have replaced domestic servants, machines have replaced animals. And, like the living things they replace, machines wear out in proportion to use. Take, for an example, your automobile: the fewer miles, the better resale value because cars wear out with usage. There may be a necessity for certain types of industry to operate seven days a week; however, a greater portion of industrial activities could shut down on the Lord's Day.

Finally, as God teaches us how to structure His day socially, He includes those outside the church. He concludes by prohibiting from work "thy stranger who is within thy gates." In Israel the sojourner or stranger was the Gentile who lived in the midst of God's people. God commands that not only His people cease from labor but also the people outside the covenant in their midst. Even though the stranger could not participate in the feasts or in temple worship, he had to cease from his work on the Sabbath.

Although the government may not legislate that people go to church, may it not legislate that businesses and shops be closed on the Lord's Day? Such laws, once prevalent in the United States and Britain, created an environment that was not only spiritually healthy but also mentally and physically beneficial.

The Westminster Shorter Catechism question 61 interprets the fourth commandment as forbidding "unnecessary thoughts, words, or works, about our worldly employments or recreations." The primary proof text is Isaiah 58:13–14, where the prophet is dealing with the lifeless formalism of the worship of God's people. He rebukes them for their formalism: clinging to sin while going through the motions of worship and substituting external acts (fasting) for true obedience. In contrast to this formalism, he sets before them the great principle of the Sabbath and the blessings of God that attend it. He says that the God of the covenant solemnly promises great spiritual blessings to those who keep the Sabbath day holy: "Then shalt thou delight thyself in the LORD; and I will cause thee to ride upon the high places of the earth, and feed thee with the heritage of Jacob thy father" (v. 14).

In verse 13, Isaiah begins negatively: "If thou turn away thy foot from the sabbath, from doing thy pleasure on my holy day." Anticipating the language of the New Testament—that Jesus is Lord of the Sabbath (Matt. 12:8) and that the New Testament Sabbath is called the Lord's Day (Rev. 1:10), Isaiah refers to the Sabbath as God's "holy day" and "the holy day of the LORD." God calls the Sabbath a holy day because He sanctified it (Gen. 2:2–3). Since it is the holy day of the Lord, we are to sanctify it. If we pursue our pleasure on the Sabbath, we trample underfoot God's holy ground. To enjoy the things promised, we must refrain from profaning the day.

How does one profane the day? By doing one's pleasure on it. This word "pleasure" is used throughout the Old Testament to describe those things in which one delights (Ps. 1:2; Isa. 44:28; 46:10; 58:3; Eccl. 3:1, 17; 8:6).[11] "Doing your pleasure" indicates those things you enjoy doing or are obligated to do the other six days: business, work, and play. By doing these things on God's holy day, you profane it. If you are to enjoy the promise of God, you must

---

11. I recognize that those who are on trips may have to eat in a public facility on the Lord's Day, even as they may have to stay in a hotel. Interestingly, the Puritans recognized this need as well. The Puritan-controlled Parliament in a 1644 bill to regulate the Sabbath added: "Provided, and be it Declared, That nothing in this Ordinance shall extend to the prohibiting or dressing of Meat in Private Families, or the dressing and sale of Victuals in a moderate way in Inns or Victualling-Houses, for the use of such as otherwise cannot be provided for." As quoted in James Dennison, *The Market Day of the Soul: The Puritan Doctrine of the Sabbath in England 1532–1700* (New York: University Press of America, 1983), 94.

not trample the day underfoot by doing your own pleasure on that day.

God, however, does not hinder our work or pleasure to thwart our happiness. Rather, He is calling us to turn aside from our pleasure in order to seek the pleasures He has in store for us in the day. Thus, He continues by telling us what to do. Positively, we are to honor and revere the day and "call the Sabbath a delight, the holy of the LORD, honorable" (Isa. 58:13). The word "delight" comes from the word used in verse 14—"to delight thyself in the LORD." It means to take exquisite pleasure. As we delight in people or beautiful things, we are to delight in the spiritual exercises of the day.

We delight in the day as we honor it. Since God has set it aside, we are to honor the day as special, the holy day of the Lord. This is what God means in the fourth commandment when He says, "Remember the Sabbath day, to keep it holy." We "remember the Sabbath day to keep it holy" by taking exquisite delight in that day and calling it honorable. How do we honor the Lord's Day? You honor the day by doing three things: "not doing thine own ways, nor finding thine own pleasure, nor speaking thine own words" (Isa. 58:13).

First, "not doing your own ways" means we are not to do our regular work. We are to cease doing our business, the affairs of our calling. Here the prophet is applying the prohibition of the fourth commandment when it says we are not to work nor are we to make others work. God has given us six days to do our business. The seventh belongs to Him. Thus, besides works of necessity (Matt. 12:1–8) or mercy (Matt. 12:9–14), we are not to pursue business.

We should not be going into the office or working in the store. We ought not to be doing homework or unnecessary housework. Nor should we cause others to work unnecessarily. This means we should avoid recreational eating out, going to the grocery store or mall, or traveling extensively. One grievous violation is Christian businesspeople and pastors flying on Sundays to be at work by Monday morning. Is such travel using the day for God's purposes?

Second, we are not to use the Lord's Day as a play day for "finding [our] own pleasure." The word "pleasure" is the same word used in the first part of the verse: "If thou turn away thy foot from… doing thy pleasure on my holy day." We are not to pursue our own pleasure by playing or recreating. Rather, we are to discover the peculiar treasure of the Sabbath. We are to take exquisite delight in what it offers. Hence, we ought not to be watching television, going to movies or ball games, or using the day for sports.

God is not opposed to fun. Moderate recreation the other six days is a gift of God. The Sabbath, however, is to be devoted to the peculiar spiritual pleasures of worship and service. We are to cease from our pleasures that we might pursue greater and nobler things. We are to look at the Lord's Day like a spiritual vacation. I look forward to a vacation as a time I can forget about job pressures and enjoy my family. God gives us a weekly vacation that we might forget earthly things and enjoy Him.

This should not be interpreted as a prohibition of all physical activity on the Lord's Day. Children need physical activity, and some adults might need some physical activity too so they will be alert for afternoon or evening worship. Plan activities such as walks on which you can talk to your children about God and the things He has made. Encourage them to act out Bible stories. Keep some good Bible games on hand.

God is not opposed to rest. But the rest of the Lord's Day is not a rest of idleness or recreation. It is a rest that enables us to enjoy the purposes of the day and equips us to serve Him the other six days. Westminster Shorter Catechism question 60 requires us to "[spend] the whole time in the publick and private exercises of God's worship, except so much as is to be taken up in the works of necessity and mercy," and some wrongly interpret this as prohibiting a nap. However, moderate physical rest may be a *work of necessity* to enable us to keep the Sabbath properly and to be refreshed for the next week.

Third, we ought to avoid unnecessary conversation about work and recreation, which Isaiah calls "speaking your own words." We are not to talk about our regular pursuits, but rather we are to set our minds on the things of the Lord. This does not rule out conversation with Christian friends about work or family affairs. In order to have true fellowship we need to know what is going on in each other's lives. Westminster Shorter Catechism question 61 gives an apt summary of the requirement of Isaiah 58:13.

> *What is forbidden in the fourth commandment?*
>
> The fourth commandment forbiddeth the omission or careless performance of the duties required and the profaning the day by idleness or doing that which is in itself sinful, or by unnecessary thoughts, words, or works about our worldly employments or recreations.

The purpose of this careful observance of the Sabbath was not to create a legalistic entanglement that stifles people, but to free the people of God for the wonderful privilege of worshiping God and enjoying Him. In light of this purpose, God's Word offers great promises with regard to the careful observance of the Lord's Day.

In Isaiah 58:14, God attaches three excellent promises to Sabbath observance. The God of the covenant solemnly promises ("for the mouth of the LORD hath spoken it") great spiritual blessings to those who keep the Sabbath day holy: "Then shalt thou delight thyself in the LORD; and I will cause thee to ride upon the high places of the earth, and feed thee with the heritage of Jacob thy father." I do not know three greater things promised in the entire Bible than what God pledges here.

First, we are promised exquisite, spiritual pleasure as we delight ourselves in the Lord. The word
"delight" means exquisite pleasure. To take exquisite
pleasure in the Lord is to be overcome by His beauty,
His glory, His attributes, and His work (Job 22:26;
Isa. 61:10); to have our hearts ravished by the truths
of the Word of God; and to have God manifest His
love to us. God is promising you a communion and
fellowship with Him that defies description. I like to
think of the Sabbath as a wonderful garden adorned
with beautiful flowers where God meets with us.

But God doesn't stop there. He adds the language of victory, taken from Deuteronomy 32:12–13
and 33:29, when He says that we will ride upon the
high places of the earth. In Deuteronomy God promises Israel great victory over her enemies. As Isaiah
speaks about returning to the land, he promises the
people victory over their enemies (Isa. 33:16). That
victorious return is a picture of the victory promised
in the new covenant. We who are members of new
Zion will have victory. In Christ we are more than
conquerors (Rom. 8:37). We will have victory over
Satan and sin. Sabbath-keeping is a means of grace
that will help us die to sin and grow in holiness.

But there is more. Not only will we delight in the
Lord with exquisite pleasure and have victory over
our enemies, but also God promises that we will
enjoy the benefits of our salvation; He promises to
"feed you with the heritage of Jacob your father."
He is promising that Israel will again possess the

land (Ps. 105:10–11). We know that possession of the land was a symbol of the inheritance of God's covenant people. What does it mean to you and me? Our inheritance includes the benefits of salvation—justification, adoption, sanctification, assurance of salvation, boldness in prayer, and our ultimate glorification. This promise means we will revel in our privileges as children of God.

How then are we to approach keeping the Lord's Day holy? The principles by which the day is to be observed are set forth in Westminster Confession 21.8:

> This sabbath is then kept holy unto the Lord, when men, after a due preparing of their hearts, and ordering of their common affairs beforehand do not only observe an holy rest all the day from their own works, words, and thoughts about their worldly employments and recreations; but also are taken up the whole time in the publick and private exercises of his worship, and in the duties of necessity and mercy.[12]

All true Sabbath-keeping begins by our actively resting in God alone for our salvation. Without actively focusing on Christ and living in dependence on Him, there is no true Sabbath-keeping. When we turn aside from our work and pleasure, we are freed to worship Him.

---

12. See also Westminster Shorter Catechism question 60.

Such worship requires preparation.[13] On Saturday evening, be sure you have finished your work and chores so that you will not be distracted by them. Be sure the car is serviced and the necessary groceries have been purchased. Prepare your clothing. Conclude the day, like all days, with some meditation and prayer, particularly focusing on the Lord's Day. Get a good night's rest.

On the Lord's Day morning, begin with thankfulness for the Lord's Day and its benefits. Seek God to grant you the things promised. Strive to stir up your affections by meditation, prayer, and listening to and singing psalms and hymns. Pray for the worship service and the preaching of the Word. Have a plan for the day: What benefits are you seeking? What service can you render? What book do you want to read? What will you do with and for your children?

Corporate worship should be at the top of your list of pleasures. If your congregation has an afternoon or evening service, be committed to returning (unless you are hindered by distance). In the afternoon, have a time for extended family worship; review the sermon, perhaps in the car as you return home after the second service; take advantage of the time in the afternoon to read and pray.

Hospitality is an essential part of fellowship and ministry, so use the day for exercising it. Be involved

---

13. In the verses from Ecclesiastes, the term translated "purpose" in the King James Version is literally "delight."

in ministries such as going to the nursing home, visiting the sick and the shut-ins, and going out to witness and distribute tracts.

Those with young children will need to tailor the day's activities around their children: reading to them, working on Scripture and catechetical memorization, and playing games with them that are appropriate to the Lord's Day. This will instill in them a great delight for this day.

Particularly, you should teach your children to participate in worship services. Work with them during the week on how to sit still and be quiet. Teach them to say "Amen" after prayers and songs (1 Cor. 14:16). Practice songs in family worship during the week that the congregation will sing in corporate worship. Have them memorize the rubrics used in worship: the Creed, the Ten Commandments, and the Doxology. Teach them how to listen to a sermon. When they are very young, have them draw a picture that picks up on something in the sermon. Help them as they grow older to pick out key words. Pastors should address them and use illustrations tailored for them. Knowing their catechism also will help them to profit from the sermon.

Sometimes your children will face challenges when friends are visiting. You can offset this by putting up toys that you do not want them to get into on the Lord's Day and by replacing them with sound Bible-related books and videos, Lord's Day games, and dress-up clothes for them to act out Bible stories.

When your children are young, you may experience the conflict of naptime; often naptimes collide with leaving for the second service. By God's grace, they will adjust to the Sunday schedule.

So is the Lord's Day for you? I hope your answer is a hearty yes! Such Sabbath-keeping has been the practice and conviction of most Reformed Christians from the time of the Reformation until about seventy-five years ago. We have a wonderful promise from our God that we will delight in Him, have victory, and enjoy our inheritance. Is there anyone who enjoys the grace of the gospel and the power of the Holy Spirit who does not want what God promises here? God solemnly swears to you, "If you want to delight in me, if you want this exquisite pleasure and victory, stop profaning My day and call it a delight. Honor it by ceasing from your own ways, from your own pleasures, and from speaking your own words. Then you will delight in the Lord." May the Lord give us all hearts to understand and wills to respond.